good things Jesus Did

Written by
Rhonda Reeves

Illustrated by
Timothy Robinson

Woman's Missionary Union
Birmingham, AL 35283-0010

Published by Woman's Missionary Union, SBC
P.O. Box 830010
Birmingham, AL 35283-0010

Dewey Decimal Classification: CE
Subject Headings: Christian Life—Children
                  Jesus Christ—CHILDREN'S LITERATURE

Series: Missions and Me

ISBN: 1-56309-285-9
W998105•069•05M1

Dedication

To the many dedicated and committed Mission Friends teachers who pour their hearts into teaching preschoolers about the good things Jesus did, thank you for caring. Thank you for sharing. *Preschoolers are worth it!*

Jesus was born in Bethlehem.

Soon Jesus grew into a boy,

and then became a strong man.

Jesus went about doing good things.

Jesus went to church.

Jesus prayed.

Jesus healed sick people.

Jesus told people about God.

Jesus liked little children.

He said, "Let the little
children come to me."

Jesus said, "You are my friends."

Jesus loves you

and wants you to love others.